# WHAT I WISH
## FOR YOU

SECOND EDITION

TO *My dear Alana* ♡     *2014*

FROM *Much love Grandma* ⊗

# WHAT I WISH FOR YOU

## 52 Heart Inspirations for Joyful Living

SECOND EDITION

ALEXANDRA
HARDY-SHAMAYA

ISSAC DAVID
GARUDA,PHD

AMADO PRESS ~ AMADO, ARIZONA

Library of Congress Control Number: 2009903836

ISBN: 978-0-9640898-1-5

Amado Press
PO Box 6335
Amado, AZ 85645
Telephone: 800-531-5956
E-mail: info@AmadoPress.com
Website: www.AmadoPress.com

Publicist: Be Mello Media, Tara Baukus Mello, 1062 Wilson Dr., Simi Valley, CA 93065
Telephone: 805-577-0610  E-Mail: tara@bemello.com

Original illustrations and cover painting by : Alexandra Hardy-Shamaya
Ten additional wishes by : Alexandra Hardy-Shamaya
Ten added illustrations by : Alexandra Hardy-Shamaya & Trey McLaughlin
Cover and Interior Design: James Bennett Design

To Matthew,
who started it all

# INTRODUCTION

This is a book born of love. Its simple but profound messages reach deep into the core of our humanity and touch us in ways that we know are true.

Isaac David Garuda, PhD, was considering how to honor his son Matthew's twenty-second birthday when he had what he calls a "heart inspiration." A succession of warm, loving wishes suddenly flooded his awareness and he wrote them to Matthew in the form of a letter.

The beautiful wishes Isaac wrote were filled with universal meaning, and the letter took on a life of its own. Alexandra Hardy-Shamaya teamed up with Isaac, creating illustrations to accompany his words, and the first edition of *What I Wish for You* was born.

*What I Wish for You* is a book to be read over and over again. It will call you to live the life you want for yourself. Read it, enjoy it, and take the messages to heart.

For this second edition, Alexandra Hardy-Shamaya has added ten wishes and drawings. These ten additional wishes enhance the original 42, completing the circle of heart inspirations.

# SECTION I

# INSPIRATION

May you dream
magnificent dreams
and awaken to make
them come true.

# DIRECTION

May you discover the true purpose of
your existence and pursue that purpose
with vigor, grace, and a very good
sense of humor.

# DESIRE

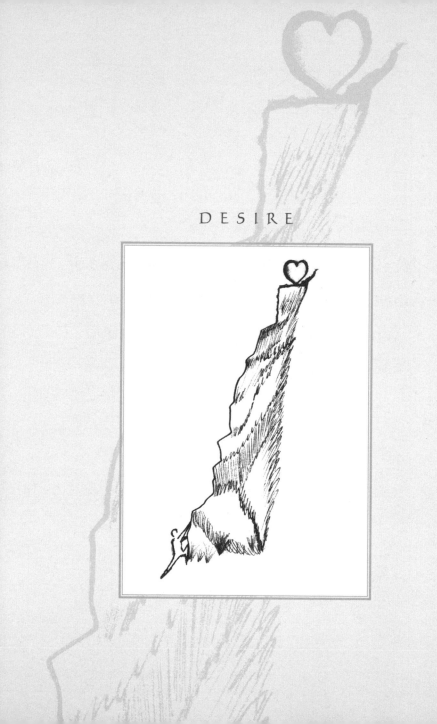

May you be blessed with
strong intentions about those things
in life you endeavor to undertake
and accomplish.

# INTENTION

May you focus on your purpose
while enjoying the spontaneous
journey to manifestation.

# WORD

## COMMITMENT

May you honor your word
with sincerity and consistent
follow through.

# COURAGE

May you stand steady
in the face of the one aspect
of life that is certain—
namely, uncertainty.

PERSEVERANCE

May you welcome obstacles
as opportunities to express
yourself in ways you didn't
think possible.

# COMPASSION

May you have a gentle heart
for yourself and others
at those times when life
is difficult.

# VITALITY

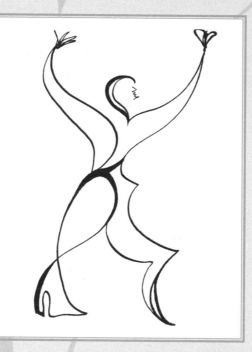

May you find plenty of
physical energy for playing
the game of life to
its fullest.

# HUMOR

May you cultivate the
ability to laugh at yourself
and eliminate the habit of
feeling sorry for yourself.

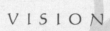

# VISION

May you see and appreciate
things as they are rather than
as they seem to be.

# INTEGRITY

May your sense of self-worth
protect you from ever pretending
to be someone or something
you are not.

PATIENCE

May you always remember
that the course of human events
rarely goes according to one's
personal timetable.

# SECTION

# 2

PASSION

May you touch
the lives of all who meet you
by the very force of your
spirit and love.

# CONFIDENCE

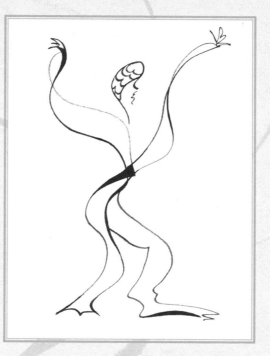

May you follow
the dictates of your heart,
regardless of what other people
may think of you.

WORK

May you find creative work
that nourishes your spirit with joy
and fills your pocketbook
with green.

# NURTURANCE

May you consistently
make time to do those things
that remind you it's great
to be you.

# SELF-POSSESSION

May you appreciate
your own company and
enjoy times of quiet
and solitude.

# INTELLIGENCE

May you see the futility of
placing blame, finding fault,
or making excuses in relation to
what you experience.

# RESPONSIBILITY

May you know yourself
as the generator of your
inner feelings as well as
your overt actions.

# INNOCENCE

May you love the child
in you that is playful, inquisitive,
sparkling, blameless, and
full of wonder.

# SELF-ACCEPTANCE

May you accept your errors
and transmute them from the
bitterness of self-blame to the
sweetness of self-love.

# BALANCE

May you bring
a sense of playfulness
as well as practicality to
all your endeavors.

# SELF-EXPRESSION

May you laugh heartily,
cry openly, sing loudly, dance wildly,
love unashamedly.

# OBJECTIVITY

May you give yourself permission
to experience and express everything
you feel as a person, without taking
anything personally.

# RECOGNITION

May you realize
what an incredible
Being you are.

# SECTION

## 3

# HEALING

May you allow the unresolved
hurts, frustrations, and fears from
the past to seek their release
in the present and thus be healed
once and for all time.

Ask for what
you want and need
and give what you can.

# ACCEPTANCE

May you embrace
without resistance a situation
that you cannot change.

# BREATH

May you feel so at home
in your body that you always
breathe deeply, easily,
and freely.

# EXCITEMENT

May your life be a stirring
ride through the mysteries of
consciousness and the
wonders of the world.

# DEPTH

May your life be filled
with people, places, and things
that touch you at the core of
your being.

# SANCTUARY

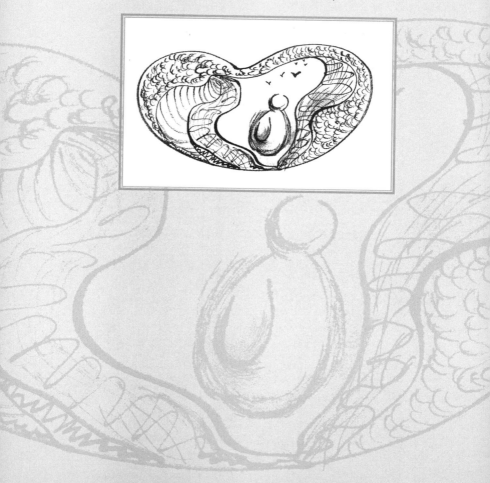

May your home
always be a place of warmth,
caring, friendship and
sharing.

# SPICE

May you lead a vivid life,
richly textured with many glorious
sights    sounds    smells
tastes    touches.

# ROMANCE

May you join with a mate
and together share as much love
and affection as anyone could
ever want.

# FRIENDSHIP

May you have many
wonderful friends who love you
just the way you are, yet challenge you
to be all that you can be.

# PRESENCE

May you abide
in the ever-changing Now,
knowing that nothing is real
but the present moment.

# WISDOM

May you let your intuitive self
become the supreme authority in your life,
and may you always trust what
you know from that self.

REVERENCE

May you value, honor, and
esteem your and every other
self as sacred units of
the one Unity.

# SECTION

# 4

May you be moved in the
direction of an oceanic experience
of the perfection and Unity
in all things.

# APPRECIATION

May you feel grateful
at all times and especially when
life is not comfortable.

TRANSFORM

May you be birthed
to a new way of being.

# TRANSMUTE

May you know that
all your experiences are a gift
even when they are
not pleasant.

# TRANSCEND

May you go beyond
the event and reside in peace,
knowing that all is in perfect order.

TRUST

May you not
burden yourself with
a need to make sense
out of everything.

FAITH

May you realize
the connection to and
oneness with your source.

# WELL-BEING

May you honor the
needs of the body and spirit
so as to experience
good health always.

# ABUNDANCE

May you tap the spiritual riches
within you, from which flows everything
you need to live the exact life
your heart desires.

# FREEDOM

May you live each moment
free of worry about the future
and regret about
the past.

# GRACE

May you experience a sense
of awe from the beauty that you see —
the humility that you feel —
in the garden of life.

MASTERY

May you realize a
wondrous, fulfilling life that
serves one paramount purpose:
the good of all that is.

JOY

And last, but not least,
may you live with
outrageous joyfulness
in all your years.

# ACKNOWLEDGMENTS

Many wonderful people have contributed to the publication
of the first edition of this book. Among them are the following:

Kendall Morse, my friend and wordsmith of the highest
order, for editing the original manuscript and turning it into
a literary piece worth publishing.

Diana Hunter, book packager, who shepherded this project
over hill and dale with sensitivity and creative energy.

Laurel Gregory, whose friendship and encouragement
launched this project out of the idea stage into a reality.

Alexandra Hardy-Shamaya, whose incredible artwork brings
so much aliveness to this book and to the world.

And finally, to my first-born son, Matthew Jacob Fischer,
whose presence in my life gave birth to *What I Wish for You*.

Thank you one and all from the bottom of my heart.

—Isaac


I, too, thank all of the original contributors and dear friends
who have believed in me and who have supported my mis-
sion to get *What I Wish for You* out to the world. I am also
very grateful to those who have contributed their talents to
the birth of the second edition.

Tara Mello, who through her multi-faceted talents and support, has forged the innovation for a second edition of *What I Wish for You*.

James Bennett, a graphic Houdini, who added dimensional depth and interest to my drawings and who designed the cover and gave *What I Wish for You* a new face that beautifully reflects its timeless messages.

To my dear husband, Mel, who has participated with me in this second edition journey and life in general, "you are my hero."

My son Trey, a gifted artist, who provided some of the drawings for this edition, and who catalyzed my spiritual awakening by providing abundant opportunities for me to grow emotionally and spiritually. I say, "thank you, you are my gift."

And, finally, all my dear friends and spiritual mentors. A special thank you to Helene Auerbach, a true example of unconditional love and a friend at all times – thank you for never judging, for accepting me as I am, for supporting my life journey, and for helping me keep *What I Wish for You* in print because you believed in its value. I thank you all for your contributions to my life and *What I Wish for You*.

—Alexandra

# FOR MORE INFORMATION

Alexandra Hardy-Shamaya is an artist and writer who invokes Spirit to guide her work. She creates transcendental paintings that touch people in profound ways through their brilliant colors and powerful symbolism, while her transformational jewelry designs are created with the intention of healing and balance. As a writer, her life is centered in her "wish work," which currently includes creating the Living the Wishes guidebook and a series of in-person and virtual workshops to assist others in "living the wishes" in *What I Wish for You*.

To learn more about Alexandra and her work, please visit www.GiveTheWishes.com.

*What I Wish for You* is also a gift to the children of the world. Ten percent of the profits from the sale of *What I Wish for You* will be donated to The Smile Train, an organization committed to freeing children of the emotional and physical trauma of cleft palate.

Changing The World One Smile At A Time.